Comptroller of the Currency
Administrator of National Banks

Fair Credit Reporting

Comptroller's Handbook

October 1996

CCE

Consumer Compliance Examination

Fair Credit Reporting

Table of Contents

Introduction	1
Background and Summary	1
Consumer Report	1
Bank as a User	2
Information from a Consumer Reporting Agency	2
Information from a Source Other Than a Consumer Reporting Agency	2
General – Required Disclosures	2
Bank as Consumer Reporting Agency	3
Bank as a Purchaser of Dealer Paper Required Disclosures	4
Investigative Consumer Report	4
Penalties and Liabilities	5
Examination Objectives	6
Examination Procedures	7
Appendix	11
A. Interagency Guidance – Questions and Answers on the Fair Credit Reporting Act	11
B. Interagency Policy Statement on Prescreening by Banks and the Fair Credit Reporting Act	31
C. OCC Opinion Letters – Fair Credit Reporting Act	34
References	45

Fair Credit Reporting

Background and Summary

The Fair Credit Reporting Act (FCRA) (15 USC 1681) became effective on April 25, 1971. The FCRA is designed to regulate the consumer reporting industry; to place disclosure obligations on users of consumer reports; and to ensure fair, timely, and accurate reporting of credit information. It also restricts the use of reports on consumers and, in certain situations, requires the deletion of obsolete information. Banks may be subject to the FCRA as:

- Credit grantors.

- Purchasers of dealer paper.

- Issuers of credit cards.

- Employers.

Generally, the FCRA does not apply to commercial transactions, including those involving agricultural credit.

It does not give any federal agency authority to issue rules or regulations having the force and effect of law. The Federal Trade Commission (FTC) has issued a commentary on the FCRA (16 CFR 600.1-600.8). That commentary provides guidance to consumer reporting agencies, customers, and consumers on the FTC interpretation of the act.

Consumer Report

The consumer report may be a written or oral communication that bears on a consumer's credit standing, credit capacity, character, general reputation, personal characteristics, or mode of living. Furthermore, it must have been used, expected to be used, or collected in whole or in part for the purposes listed in 15 USC 1681a(d). A report containing information only about transactions and experiences between the consumer and the institution making the report is not a consumer report.

Bank as a User

Few banks are consumer reporting agencies. Most banks are users of information obtained from them. As a user, a bank must identify itself to the consumer reporting agency and certify that the information requested will be used as specified in the act and for no other purpose. A written blanket certification may be given by the bank to cover all inquiries to a particular consumer reporting agency.

Banks also rely on information from sources other than consumer reporting agencies. As a user, a bank must disclose different information depending on its source.

Information from a Consumer Reporting Agency

If consumer credit is denied or the cost of credit is increased, partially or wholly on the basis of information from a consumer reporting agency, the bank must disclose, orally or in writing, that information in the report was used in the credit decision. It must inform the consumer of the name and address of the consumer reporting agency from which it received the information. It is recommended that the disclosure be made in writing.

Information from a Source Other Than a Consumer Reporting Agency

If consumer credit is denied or the cost of credit is increased, partially or wholly on the basis of information obtained from a source other than a consumer reporting agency, the user must disclose the applicant's right to file a written request for the nature of the information within 60 days of learning of the adverse action. Alternatively, the bank may disclose the nature of the information and must do so, if it receives a request from the consumer. That information should be sufficiently detailed to enable the consumer to evaluate its accuracy. The source of the information need not be, but may be, disclosed. In some instances, it may be impossible to identify the nature of certain information without also revealing the source.

General – Required Disclosures

The obligations imposed on users of credit information are intended to allow applicants to correct erroneous reports. The disclosures are triggered by either a denial of credit or an increase in its cost. If credit is approved, but for a lesser amount than the original request, a denial under the FCRA has occurred.

The disclosures required of users of credit information also apply to outside information on comakers, guarantors, or sureties. Disclosures should be made to the party to whom they relate.

In addition, denial of an overdraft or refusal to authorize a credit card purchase based on information from any outside source would trigger the need for disclosures, assuming the information bears upon the consumer's creditworthiness, credit standing, credit capacity, character, general reputation, personal characteristics, or mode of living.

The requirements for disclosures by users of information apply to the general type of consumer credit transactions covered by Regulation Z.

Banks may disclose orally the information required under the FCRA. However, if the action resulting in a denial of credit under the FCRA also meets the definition of adverse action under Regulation B (12 CFR 202.2(c)), the bank must make additional written disclosures to the consumer (Regulation B – 12 CFR 202.9). The required disclosures for both the FCRA and Regulation B may be provided on the same disclosure form, but they are independent and one cannot substitute for the other. To meet the requirements of both the FCRA and Regulation B, banks may wish to use form letters, copies of which may be kept in files with the completed application forms. That practice allows internal monitoring of compliance and provides evidence in the event of litigation.

Bank as Consumer Reporting Agency

The term consumer reporting agency applies to any organization that might render a consumer report as defined previously. Certain banks function as consumer reporting agencies and, to the extent that they issue consumer reports, are covered by the FCRA. A bank may become a consumer reporting agency if it regularly furnishes information about a consumer to, for example, other creditors, correspondents, holding companies, or affiliates, other than information on its own transactions or experiences. However, if the bank furnishes information from outside sources to another party involved in the same transaction, it does not become a consumer reporting agency. For instance, such parties could include an insurer or a guarantor (as in the case of Federal Housing Administration, VA, or private insurers or insured student loan programs), and other financial institutions participating in the transaction, or a collection agency engaged in collecting on the transaction. All consumer reporting agencies must:

- Make required disclosures to consumers upon request and proper identification.

- Ensure that obsolete information is not reported.

- Resolve accuracy disputes with customers.

- Provide reports only for legitimate purposes.

- Keep a dated record of each recipient of information about a consumer, even when the inquiry is oral.

- Train personnel sufficiently to explain information furnished to customers.

Bank as a Purchaser of Dealer Paper Required Disclosures

The bank must make to the consumer disclosures required of a user, whenever it, because of information from an outside source, denies or increases the cost of credit requested by a merchant to be extended directly or indirectly to a consumer. However, the merchant must have advised the consumer of the bank's name and address before contacting it to prevent the bank from becoming a consumer reporting agency.

Investigative Consumer Report

When an investigative consumer report is requested from a consumer reporting agency, the bank must inform the consumer not later than three days after such request that a report may be made. An investigative consumer report is one in which a consumer's character, general reputation, personal characteristics, or mode of living is ascertained by interviewing persons who may know him or her. The consumer also must be informed that a written request may be made for the nature and scope of the investigation. If a request is received, the bank has five days to furnish the required information.

Penalties and Liabilities

Banks may be liable for negligent noncompliance as either users of information or as consumer reporting agencies. Civil liability may include actual damages, court costs, and attorney's fees. In addition, the court may award punitive damages in cases of willful noncompliance. Any bank officer or employee who obtains a credit report under false pretenses will be subject to a penalty of not more than $5,000 or imprisonment of not more than one year, or both.

1. To appraise the quality of the bank's compliance management system for the Fair Credit Reporting Act (FCRA).

2. To determine the reliance that can be placed on the bank's compliance management system, including internal controls and procedures performed by the person(s) responsible for monitoring the bank's compliance review function for the FCRA.

3. To determine the bank's compliance with the FCRA.

4. To initiate corrective action when policies or internal controls are deficient, or when violations of law or regulation are identified.

1. From the examiner who completed the Compliance Management System program, obtain information pertinent to the area of examination (historical examination findings, complaint information, and significant findings from compliance review/audit).

2. Through discussions with management and review of the following documents, determine whether the bank's internal controls are adequate to ensure compliance in the area under review.

    ☐ Organizational charts.
    ☐ Process flowcharts.
    ☐ Policies and procedures.
    ☐ Loan documentation and disclosures.
    ☐ Checklists/worksheets and review documents.
    ☐ Computer programs.

    Identify procedures used daily to detect errors/violations promptly. Also review the procedures used to ensure compliance when changes occur (e.g., changes in software programs).

3. Review compliance review/audit work papers and determine whether:

    a. The procedures used address all regulatory provisions (see section on transactional testing).

    b. Steps are taken to follow up on previously identified deficiencies.

    c. The procedures used include samples that cover all product types and decision centers.

    d. The work performed is accurate (through a review of some transactions).

    e. Significant deficiencies and their root causes are included in reports to management/board.

f.   Corrective actions are timely and appropriate.

g.   The area is reviewed at an appropriate interval.

Transactional Testing

4.   Select a sample of rejected loan application files and determine whether:

   a.   The bank, as a user, makes the required disclosures (15 USC 1681m(a)).

   b.   The bank has procedures to inform consumers (upon request) of the nature of the other outside information (15 USC 1681m(b)).

5.   Determine whether the bank's procedures are adequate to ensure that consumer reports are obtained only for a permissible purpose.

6.   If the bank is a consumer reporting agency, determine if procedures ensure that:

   a.   Required disclosures are made to consumers upon request and proper identification (15 USC 1681g).

   b.   Obsolete information is not reported (15 USC 1681c).

   c.   Accuracy disputes are resolved with the customer (15 USC 1681i).

   d.   Reports are provided only for permissible purposes (15 USC 1681b).

   e.   Proper records are maintained on each recipient of information about the consumer (15 USC 1681g(a)(3)).

   f.   Personnel are trained adequately to furnish information (15 USC 1681h(c)).

   g.   Procedures are maintained to assure the maximum possible accuracy of information received, recorded, and reproduced (15 USC 1681e(b)).

Conclusions

7. Summarize here all violations of law, regulation, or ruling and use when making SMS entries. (Refer to EC 263, "SMS Documentation Policy.")

Citation	Department	Violation	Recommendation	Policy Guide	Reference
a. ____	____	____	____	____	____
b. ____	____	____	____	____	____
c. ____	____	____	____	____	____
d. ____	____	____	____	____	____
e. ____	____	____	____	____	____

8. If the violation(s) noted above represent(s) a pattern or practice, determine the root cause by identifying weaknesses in internal controls, compliance review, training, management oversight, or other factors. Consider whether civil money penalties (CMP), suspicious transaction reporting, or an enforcement action should be recommended (see CMP matrix).

9. Identify action needed to correct violations and weaknesses in the bank's compliance system, as appropriate. Form a conclusion about the reliability of the compliance system for the area under review and provide conclusions to the examiner performing the compliance management system program.

10. Determine, in consultation with the examiner-in-charge, if violations or deficiencies in the compliance system are significant enough to merit bringing them to the board's attention in the report of examination. If so, prepare items for inclusion under the heading Matters Requiring Board Attention and under a Type 75 Follow-up Analysis.

11. Determine whether any items identified during this examination could materialize into a supervisory concern before the next on-site examination. (Consideration should be given to any planned increase in activity in this area, planned personnel changes, planned policy changes,

planned changes to outside auditors or consultants, planned changes in business strategy, etc.) If so, summarize your concerns and assess the potential risk to the institution and discuss with the examiner-in-charge and/or appropriate bank personnel.

12. Discuss findings with bank management and obtain a commitment(s) to corrective action.

Interagency Guidance – Questions and Answers on the Fair Credit Reporting Act

The following questions and answers deal with the applicability of the Fair Credit Reporting Act to a financial institution's operations. They are designed to help institutions understand the act and its requirements and apply them to the operations of institutions subject to the enforcement authority of the Office of the Comptroller of the Currency, the Federal Deposit Insurance Corporation, the Office of Thrift Supervision, and the Federal Reserve Board. Answers should be read in the context of the other questions and answers, which often relate to each other. Although the questions and answers refer to banks, that term is intended to include all financial institutions.

In some instances, the act's applicability to institutions is unclear. As a result, information in these questions and answers should not be relied on without advice of counsel. However, the OCC will regard institutions that comply with these guidelines as complying with the act.

Bank as a User of Consumer Reports

1.   May a bank obtain a consumer report from a consumer reporting agency for a loan application?

     Yes. Reports may be obtained for this and other legitimate business purposes and for the review or collection of an account, employment, or insurance underwriting (16 CFR 604 – see question 25 for a list of permissible purposes).

2.   Are there new procedures required to obtain a consumer report?

     Yes. The bank must identify itself and certify to the reporting agency (consumer reporting agency) the purposes for which the information is sought. It must also certify that the information will be used for no other purpose (16 CFR 607).

3. Must certification be given each time a consumer report is requested?

    No. A written blanket certification by the bank could cover all inquiries to a particular consumer reporting agency.

4. Does a bank that uses a consumer report have any new responsibilities to the consumer?

    Yes. A bank must make disclosures to the consumer if it denies employment or credit or insurance for personal, family, or household purposes, or increases the cost, even partially because of information in a consumer report from a consumer reporting agency. It must advise the consumer orally or in writing that information in the report caused or contributed to the denial or increase in cost, and state the name and address of the consumer reporting agency issuing the report. The bank is not required to disclose the nature of the information in the report (16 CFR 615(a) – see question 56, which deals with the denial of employment based on a consumer report).

5. What would constitute a denial of credit?

    If the credit is subject to any condition (that is, credit would not have been extended without it) because of information in the consumer report, there is a denial that would require disclosures. Such cases are the requirement of a larger down payment, a shorter maturity, a co-signer, guarantor, or additional collateral. If a consumer applies, for example, for a credit card limit of $1,500 and only $1,000 is approved because of information in a consumer report, a denial has occurred.

6. Is a bank responsible to the consumer when it obtains information from someone other than a consumer reporting agency?

    Yes. Disclosures must be made when credit for personal, family, or household purposes is denied or the charge is increased even partly because of information obtained from someone other than a consumer reporting agency bearing on the consumer's creditworthiness, credit standing, credit capacity, character, general reputation, personal characteristics, or mode of living. Disclosure would not be required if the denial is based on the bank's own experience with the consumer, on his/her credit application, or on the bank's credit policies. Required disclosures must be made regardless of whether the information is fresh or in the files. At the time credit is denied or the charge increased, the bank must inform the consumer orally or in writing of his/her right to make a written request for disclosure of the nature of the information. If the consumer requests this information within 60 days, the bank must tell him/her the nature of the information orally or in writing. Note that these requirements apply to credit and not to insurance or employment when disclosures are required and a report from a consumer reporting agency is involved (16 CFR 615(b) – see question 4).

7. What would the nature of the information include?

The information would include that the consumer's: credit history with another bank is poor; income is not what it is represented to be; period of employment, as specified on the application, is inaccurate; address is incorrect; debts are greater than represented; and statement that his/her debts are current is inaccurate. The nature of the information should be sufficient to enable the consumer to question its accuracy if he/she believes it is erroneous.

8. Is the source disclosed when stating the nature of the information?

The source may need to be disclosed to identify the nature of certain information but it is not required.

9. Do the disclosure requirements discussed in questions 4 through 8 apply to information about a comaker, guarantor, or surety?

Yes. Those disclosures should be made to the comaker, guarantor, or surety to whom the information relates.

10. Do those rules apply when a bank decides not to honor an overdraft on a checking account, because of information from a third party?

Yes. Disclosures must be made if an overdraft is denied because of information from any outside source. This is so whether the account ordinarily includes overdraft credit privileges (for example, check credit). No disclosures must be made if the denial is based on the bank's general policy not to honor overdrafts.

11. Must disclosures be made when a bank that issues credit cards refuses to honor a credit card or to authorize a merchant to honor one, because of information received from any outside source?

Yes. The issuer must disclose the name and address of the consumer reporting agency, or the consumer's right to know the nature of the information when it was received from someone other than a consumer reporting agency. In the latter instance, when a merchant is involved, it appears that the retailer must make disclosures on the issuer's behalf, since the consumer must receive notice of his/her right "at the time such adverse action is communicated to the consumer." However, if the information does not bear upon the customer's creditworthiness, credit standing, credit capacity, character, general reputation, personal characteristics, or mode of living (for example, if the information is merely that the card is lost, stolen, or being used in an unauthorized manner), or if the information is not obtained from an outside source, disclosures would not be required.

12. Do these disclosure requirements apply to business or commercial transactions?

No. The user requirements of disclosure apply only in connection with employment or for credit or insurance for personal, family, or household purposes. For credit, they apply to the general type of consumer credit transactions covered by Regulation Z.

13. Must a bank make any disclosure to the consumer when it denies credit or increases the charges solely on the basis of its prior transactions or experiences with him or her, or unverified information furnished by the consumer on his or her application?

No. Disclosure is not required in these circumstances. However, disclosures must be made if credit is denied or the cost increased because of information obtained from third parties when verifying information on the application (16 CFR 603(d)(3)(A)).

14. Must disclosures be made if one bank department or branch obtains information on the consumer from another department or branch of the same bank as to its prior transactions or experiences, and denies credit or increases the charge based on this information?

No. Disclosures are required only when information is obtained from an outside source. However, disclosures must be made if the department or branch transmitting the information relays information obtained from third parties outside the bank, and the bank either denies or increases the cost of credit based upon the information.

15. What actions should a bank consider to ensure its compliance with the requirements imposed on a user of consumer reports?

The bank should consider: filing the certification mentioned in question 2 with each consumer reporting agency whose services may be used; retaining a file copy; instructing employees that consumer reports may be obtained only for the purposes specified in the act and certification; developing procedures for making required disclosures to consumers when credit, insurance, or employment is denied, or when the cost of credit or insurance is increased, based on information obtained from outside sources; and recording all inquiries to reporting agencies or others, as well as information obtained through those inquiries, so that accurate disclosure can be made to consumers.

Forms may be useful for advising the consumer of the name and address of the consumer reporting agency (when a consumer report is involved), or his/her rights to request the nature of the information when other outside sources are involved.

Bank as a Consumer Reporting Agency

16. Can a bank be a consumer reporting agency?

Yes. If the bank regularly furnishes information in its files about a consumer, other than information solely about its transactions or experiences with the consumer, it may be considered a consumer reporting agency. A consumer reporting agency is any entity that, for monetary fees or dues, or on a cooperative nonprofit basis, regularly engages in whole or in part in the practice of assembling or evaluating consumer credit information or other information on consumers to furnish consumer reports to third parties, and that uses any means or facility of interstate commerce to prepare or furnish consumer reports (16 CFR 603(d) and (f)).

17. Does this apply to the regular exchange of information among correspondent banks, between a holding company and its subsidiaries, or among subsidiaries of a holding company?

Yes. However, a branch or department of a bank may furnish information to another branch or department of that bank without becoming a consumer reporting agency.

18. What information may a bank give to third parties in response to inquiries about a consumer, without becoming a consumer reporting agency?

The bank may relate information solely about its transactions or experiences with the consumer. For example, the bank may disclose that the consumer had a history of delinquency and could give other information about the status of any loans or deposits with it. To ensure that it does not become a consumer reporting agency, it should not regularly issue information:

- Contained in credit applications bearing on the consumer's creditworthiness, credit standing, credit capacity, character, general reputation, personal characteristics, or mode of living.

- Obtained in reports from consumer reporting agencies or any other information obtained from third parties. For example, a bank that obtained information as a user may become a consumer reporting agency if it subsequently conveys the information to another bank.

19. Does a bank become a consumer reporting agency by transmitting information obtained from outside sources to another party involved in the same transaction?

No. The bank would not become a consumer reporting agency since it is a joint user of the same information with the other party involved in the same transaction. For example, a bank does not become a consumer reporting agency by transmitting such information to an insurer or guarantor (as in the case of the Federal Housing Administration (FHA), Veterans Administration (VA), private insurers, or insured student loan programs) to a participating bank in connection with the same transaction, or to a collection agency in connection with its efforts to collect on the transaction. Furthermore, the procurement and transmission of a consumer report to FHA, VA, or other similar insuring or guaranteeing entity is to determine whether the entity will issue its insurance or guaranty to the holder of an obligation and not whether it will issue insurance to the consumer involved.

20. If a bank regularly obtains information for its customers about the sufficiency of funds to cover checks on drawee banks and gives the information to such customers, does it become a consumer reporting agency?

No.

21. If a bank becomes a consumer reporting agency, are there any restrictions on the type of information that may be furnished?

Yes. Certain obsolete information may not be furnished by a consumer reporting agency. According to the act, the following subjects are obsolete:

- Bankruptcies that antedate the report by more than 10 years.

- Suits and judgments, paid tax liens, and accounts placed for collection or charged to profit and loss that antedate the report by more than seven years.

- Arrests, indictments, or convictions of crime that antedate the report by more than seven years.

- Any adverse information that antedates the report by more than seven years.

(Refer to 16 CFR 605 for information on when the time periods begin to run.)

22. Are there any situations in which these restrictions on obsolete information do not apply?

Yes. They do not apply in connection with a credit transaction expected to involve $50,000 or more in principal, or the underwriting of insurance that is expected to involve a face amount of $50,000 or more. They also do not apply to information for employment at an annual salary of $20,000 or more (16 CFR 605(b)).

23. Must a bank that is a consumer reporting agency remove this obsolete information from its own files after the 7-year and 10-year periods, although it wishes to use the information solely for its own use?

   No. It need not remove the information from its files. However, by not removing it, the bank may be exposed to civil liability in the event that prohibited information is negligently released (16 CFR 617).

24. What are the responsibilities of a bank that regularly furnishes information other than that about its own transactions and experiences with a consumer and thus becomes a consumer reporting agency?

   It must maintain procedures to ensure that the obsolete information specified in the act is not released, except when permitted (see question 22) in 16 CFR 604. Reasonable procedures also are necessary to ensure maximum possible accuracy of the information in any consumer report. Certifications must be obtained from all users of the information in any consumer report that it will be used only for authorized purposes and must not be released if the agency has any reasonable doubt that it will not be used. The identity of new users must be verified for authorized purposes. In addition, a consumer reporting agency has other responsibilities to consumers, as discussed under the next subhead (16 CFR 604, 605, and 607).

25. What are the authorized purposes for which consumer reports can be furnished?

   Reports may be furnished only:

   • In response to a court order.

   • According to the written instructions of the consumer to whom it relates.

- For an extension of credit involving the consumer (or review or collection of the consumer's account).

- For employment purposes.

- For the underwriting of insurance.

- For a determination of the consumer's eligibility for a license or other benefit granted by a governmental instrumentality in which the determination of an applicant's financial responsibility or status is required by law.

- For any other legitimate business need in connection with a business transaction involving the consumer (for example, on a consumer who wishes to establish a checking account in the bank, or for a builder checking the financial condition of a prospective buyer) (16 CFR 604).

26. In what other situations may a consumer reporting agency furnish information?

It may also furnish identifying information to a governmental agency for other purposes. The information is such cases is limited to the consumer's name, address, employment, and former addresses and places of employment (16 CFR 608).

Bank's Duties as a Consumer Reporting Agency

27. Does a bank that is a consumer reporting agency have responsibilities to consumers for the information it has on file?

Yes. Upon the request and proper identification of any consumer, the bank must disclose the nature and substance of all information, except medical, that it has in its files. In addition, it must disclose the sources of the information, except in the case of investigative consumer reports as noted in question 49. The bank also must disclose the recipients of any consumer report within six months preceding the request (two years in the case of reports furnished for employment purposes). Accordingly, a bank that is a consumer reporting agency should keep a dated record of each recipient of information about a consumer, even when the inquiry is oral (16 CFR 609).

28. Must the consumer specifically request disclosure of sources and recipients of reports?

No. A consumer's general request about information in his or her file requires disclosure of the nature and substance of the information, as well as sources and recipients.

29. Are there any limitations on when disclosures must be made to consumers?

Yes. Disclosure must be made only during normal business hours and only on reasonable notice by the consumer (16 CFR 610(a)).

30. Can the consumer require that disclosure be made either in person or by telephone?

Yes. Disclosures must be made if the consumer appears in person and furnishes proper identification. Disclosures also must be made by telephone if the consumer makes a written request for telephone disclosure and properly identifies himself or herself. In making disclosures by telephone, the bank can require that any toll charge be borne by the consumer (16 CFR 610(b)).

31. If the consumer asks for disclosure in person, can he/she be accompanied by another party?

Yes. He/she can be accompanied by one other person, who must furnish reasonable identification. The consumer may be required to furnish a written statement granting permission to the bank to discuss the customer's file in that person's presence (16 CFR 160(d)).

32. How must disclosures be made to the consumer?

Disclosures may be made either in writing or orally. If given orally, the consumer or his/her representative should be given reasonable opportunity to note down the information being disclosed.

33. Must the bank explain the information in the consumer's file?

Yes. It must provide trained personnel to explain any information furnished to the consumer (16 CFR 610(c)).

34. What is the meaning of the consumer's file?

It means all of the information on that consumer (bearing on his creditworthiness, credit standing, credit capacity, character, general reputation, personal characteristics, or mode of living) recorded and retained by the bank, regardless of how the information is stored. Any bank that is a consumer reporting agency under the act should maintain a central file of information on the consumer, or be capable of collecting all the information it might have on the consumer in its various departments or branches for disclosure to the consumer (16 CFR 603(g)).

35. Can the bank charge the consumer for making disclosures to him/her in connection with his/her file?

Yes, depending on the time when the consumer requests information about his/her file. If he/she makes the request either within 30 days after receiving notice that a user of a consumer report has denied or increased the charge for credit or insurance (or denied employment) on the basis of the report, or within 30 days of notification from a debt collection agency affiliated with the bank that the consumer's credit rating may be, or has been, adversely affected, the information must be furnished free of charge. However, the bank may impose a reasonable charge for making disclosures to the consumer if the request is not made within the 30-day time limit and the bank notifies the customer of the charge before making disclosures (16 CFR 612).

Disputes about a Consumer's File

36. What must a bank that is a consumer reporting agency do when a consumer questions the completeness or accuracy of information in his/her file?

The bank must, within a reasonable period of time, reinvestigate and record the current status of the questioned information, unless it has reasonable grounds to believe that the dispute is frivolous or irrelevant. The act provides that the presence of information in the consumer's file contradicting his/her contention does not, in and of itself, constitute reasonable grounds for believing the dispute is frivolous or irrelevant.

37. What must the bank do if reinvestigation indicates that the information was inaccurate, or if it can no longer be verified?

    The information must be deleted promptly from the file (16 CFR 611(a)).

38. What if reinvestigation appears to confirm the information?

    If reinvestigation does not resolve the dispute, the consumer is entitled to file a brief statement setting forth the nature of the dispute. This statement may be limited to 100 words, if the bank assists the consumer in writing a clear summary of the dispute. Unless there are reasonable grounds to believe that the dispute is frivolous or irrelevant, all subsequent consumer reports containing the information in question must clearly note that it is disputed by the consumer, and must provide either the consumer's statement or a clear and accurate summary of it (16 CFR 611(b) and (c)).

39. Must the bank notify past recipients of reports on the consumer when disputed information is deleted or a statement or notification of the dispute is filed by the consumer?

    Yes. The consumer may ask a bank that is a consumer reporting agency to provide previous recipients with notification that the information has been deleted, or a copy of the statement, codification, or summary of the dispute. It must be given to any person specifically designated by the consumer who has received a consumer report containing the disputed information within the preceding two years for employment purposes, or within the preceding six months for any other purpose (16 CFR 611(d)).

40. Must the bank disclose the consumer's right to request this notification to previous recipients?

    Yes. The bank must orally or in writing clearly and conspicuously disclose to the consumer his/her right to make the request. The disclosure must be made when, or before, the information is deleted or the consumer's statement on the disputed information is received (16 CFR 611(d)).

41. May a bank charge the consumer when it furnishes notification of deleted or disputed material to previous recipients for his/her report?

Yes, depending on when the consumer makes the request, whether the bank normally charges users of reports for furnishing them, and whether the material is found to be inaccurate or unverifiable. If the consumer makes the request either within 30 days after receiving notice that a user of a report has denied or increased the charge for credit or insurance (or denied employment) because of the report, or within 30 days of notification from a debt collection agency affiliated with the bank that the consumer's credit rating may be, or has been, adversely affected, the information must be furnished free of charge. If the request is received after 30 days, a charge may be made for furnishing notification to previous recipients. The amount must be indicated to the consumer before furnishing the information, and it may not exceed the charge that the bank would impose on each designated recipient for a consumer report. If the bank makes no such charge, then it may not charge the consumer for furnishing information about the dispute to previous recipients. In any event, the statute prohibits the imposition of any charge for notifying previous recipients about deletions of information that is found to be inaccurate or unverifiable (16 CFR 612).

Bank as a Purchaser of Dealer Paper

42. Does a bank that regularly purchases dealer paper have specific responsibilities for those transactions?

Yes, if the bank wishes to avoid becoming a consumer reporting agency. When a dealer calls the bank before credit is extended to inquire whether it will either extend credit directly to his customer or purchase the retail contract, and the bank denies the credit or increases the cost, even partly because of information from outside sources, the dealer and the bank each must make certain disclosures to the consumer to keep the bank from being considered a consumer reporting agency.

Whenever such a request is made, the dealer must advise the consumer of the name and address of the bank. If the bank denies credit or increases its cost, it must follow the normal procedures of a user of information from outside sources. If the bank's decision was based on a report from a consumer reporting agency, it must give the consumer the name and address of the agency. If its decision was based on information from a third party that is not a consumer reporting agency, the bank must disclose to the consumer his/her right to make a written request to the bank within 60 days for disclosure of the nature of the information.

If the decision to deny credit or increase its cost is based on the bank's previous experience with the consumer or its general credit policy (for example, size of down payment or maturity required), it would not need to make any disclosure to the consumer. However, a denial requiring disclosures occurs when any condition is imposed on the dealer contract on the basis of information from any outside source. This may include increasing the discount or dealer reserve or taking the paper with recourse. It also may include requiring a larger down payment, shorter maturity, a co-signer, or guarantor (16 CFR 603(d)(3)(C) and 615).

43. If, subsequent to an extension of credit to a consumer, a bank sells the consumer's obligation to a third party (including a collection agency) and furnishes information on the consumer that was obtained from outside sources to the third party in connection with that sale, does the bank become a consumer reporting agency?

No. Such a transaction is a business transaction that is generally beyond the scope of the act.

Investigative Consumer Reports

44. What is an investigative consumer report?

It is a consumer report compiled from personal interviews, with neighbors, friends, associates, or others, about the consumer's character, general reputation, personal characteristics, or mode of living (16 CFR 603(e)).

45. What are the responsibilities of a bank as a user of an investigative consumer report?

When such a report is requested from a consumer reporting agency, the bank must, within three days, mail or deliver to the consumer written notice that an investigative report, including information about his/her character, general reputation, personal characteristics, and mode of living may be made. He/she must also be informed that he/she may make a written request for the nature and scope of the investigation. If the consumer makes a written request within a reasonable period of time, the bank must make a complete and accurate disclosure of the nature and scope of the investigation. One way to do this (although not required by law) would be to furnish the consumer with a copy of any questionnaires to be used in the investigation. Within five days after the consumer's request (or within five days after the time the report was first requested by the bank, whichever is later), these disclosures must be made in writing by mailing them or otherwise delivering them to the consumer (16 CFR 603(e), 606, and 609(a)(2)).

46. Are disclosures always required when investigative consumer reports are used?

No. They are not applicable when the report is to be used for employment purposes and the consumer has not specifically applied for the position. In addition, they are not required if the bank conducts an investigation for its own purposes, using its own employees (16 CFR 606(a)(2)).

47. What if a bank denies credit, insurance, employment, or increases the charge for credit or insurance because of information in an investigative consumer report?

The bank must make the user disclosures described in the first section of this handbook, Bank as a User of Consumer Reports.

48. Are there special requirements for a bank that is a consumer reporting agency if it prepares an investigative consumer report for a third party?

Yes. Adverse information (other than public record information) in such a report cannot be included in a subsequent consumer report unless verified in the process of making the subsequent report or unless received within the three months preceding the date the subsequent report is furnished (16 CFR 614).

49. If a consumer requests disclosure of information in his/her file, must the bank reveal the nature and substance of the information contained in the investigative consumer report?

   Yes. However, if information is acquired solely for an investigative consumer report and is used for no other purpose, the source need not be disclosed (16 CFR 609(a)(2)).

Consumer Reports Furnished for Employment Purposes

50. Can a bank give out information on a consumer in response to an inquiry about him or her for employment purposes?

   Yes. However, if it regularly furnishes information other than that about its own transactions or experiences with the person, it may become a consumer reporting agency (16 CFR 603(d) and 604).

51. What is the definition of a report used for employment purposes?

   It means a report used to evaluate a consumer for employment, promotion, reassignment, or retention as an employee (16 CFR 603(h)).

52. Do the restrictions on furnishing obsolete information apply to that furnished by a bank for employment purposes if it is a consumer reporting agency?

   Yes, except when the information will be used for the employment of a person at an annual salary which equals, or which may reasonably be expected to equal, $20,000 or more. In that case, the restrictions on obsolete information do not apply (16 CFR 605(b)).

53. Are there special requirements if a bank that is a consumer reporting agency furnishes a report for employment purposes that contains matters of public record (such as liens, judgments, pending law suits, arrests,

convictions) likely to have an adverse effect on the consumer's ability to obtain employment?

Yes. At the time the information is reported to the user, the bank must notify the consumer that public record information is being reported, together with the name and address of the person to whom it is being reported.

As an alternative, the bank need not make these disclosures if it maintains strict procedures designed to ensure that, whenever public record information that is likely to have an adverse effect on a consumer's ability to obtain employment is reported, it is complete and up-to-date. The statute provides that items of public record relating to arrests, indictments, convictions, suits, tax liens, and outstanding judgments shall be considered up-to-date if the bank reports the current public record status of the item at the time the report is submitted (16 CFR 613).

54. In evaluating a potential employee, may a bank obtain a consumer report from a consumer reporting agency or other information from present or former employers?

Yes. However, banks insured by the Federal Deposit Insurance Corporation and seeking to meet the requirements of section 19 of the Federal Deposit Insurance Act (12 USC 1829) should not rely entirely on a consumer report to obtain information about whether a person has been convicted of a crime involving dishonesty or breach of trust. Information relating to such crimes is relevant to meeting the requirements of section 19 regardless of when the conviction occurred, whereas such information, if older than seven years, will probably not be contained in a report from a consumer reporting agency, unless the report will be used in connection with employment at an annual salary of $20,000 or more.

55. Must the consumer be notified if the report takes the form of an investigative consumer report?

Generally, yes, if the bank requests the report from a consumer reporting agency. However, notification would not be required if the report is obtained in connection with employment, promotion, or reassignment for which the consumer has not specifically applied. Otherwise, he/she must be notified of the request for an investigative report within three days of the request, and the bank must otherwise comply with section 606, as outlined in questions 45, 46, and 47.

56. Does the bank have any responsibilities to the prospective employee if employment is denied on the basis of a consumer report?

Yes. If information in a consumer report from a consumer reporting agency contributes at all to a denial of employment, the person must be given the name and address of the consumer reporting agency making the report. However, if employment is denied because of information from a source other than a consumer reporting agency, no disclosures are necessary (16 CFR 615).

Penalties, Liabilities, and the Act's Effect on State Law

57. What are the civil liabilities for failing to comply with the Fair Credit Reporting Act (FCRA)?

The act provides civil liabilities for either willfully or negligently failing to comply with the requirements of the FCRA. The liabilities apply to banks as users of consumer reports and as consumer reporting agencies where they are acting in that capacity. In the case of negligent noncompliance, a bank may be liable to the consumer for any actual damages sustained by the consumer, court costs, and reasonable attorney's fees. If the failure to comply is willful, a bank also may be liable to the consumer for punitive damages (16 CFR 616 and 617).

58. Is there any protection when a bank that is a user has made a good faith attempt to comply?

Yes. A user of information will not be held liable if the bank shows by a preponderance of evidence that at the time of an alleged violation it maintained reasonable procedures to ensure compliance (16 CFR 606(c) and 615(c)).

59. What is the statute of limitations on civil liability?

    Any action must be brought within two years of the date on which the liability arises, except when there has been a material and willful misrepresentation, in which case the action may be brought within two years of the misrepresentation's discovery by the consumer (16 CFR 618).

60. Are there any criminal penalties?

    Yes. The act provides for a fine of not more than $5,000 or imprisonment of not more than one year, or both, for any person who willfully and knowingly obtains information from a consumer reporting agency under false pretenses. The same criminal penalty can be imposed on any officer or employee of a bank that is a consumer reporting agency who willfully and knowingly provides information from a bank's files about a consumer to a person not authorized to receive it (16 CFR 619 and 620).

61. What effect does the act have upon state law?

    This act does not exempt any person subject to the provisions of this act from complying with the laws of any state for the collection, distribution, or use of any information on consumers, except to the extent that those laws are inconsistent with any provisions of this act, and only to the extent of the inconsistency (16 CFR 622).

Interagency Policy Statement on Screening by Banks and the Fair Credit Reporting Act

Definition

Screening (also known as "prescreening") is a process by which a consumer reporting agency (credit bureau) compiles or edits a list of consumers meeting specific credit-granting criteria provided by a bank. The list goes to the bank or a third party acting for the bank (for example, a mailing service), which uses it in soliciting specific consumers for credit products.

A screened list is the culmination of a series of consumer reports. Each consumer named on the list meets certain criteria for creditworthiness.

FCRA Rules

Although the FCRA does not expressly authorize it, screening is permissible if the bank follows certain rules. The act permits screening if the bank makes a firm offer of credit to each consumer whose name appears on the screened list. To obtain a consumer report, the bank must have a permissible purpose under the FCRA. Section 604(3)(A) of the FCRA permits a bank to obtain a consumer report if it intends to use the information to extend credit to the consumer. (Screening cannot be used to solicit responses for insurance, employment, or other purposes.) Therefore, a bank cannot use a screened list solely to send promotional material.

FCRA is intended to safeguard the confidentiality of consumer credit information. The statute requires a clear connection between the creditor and consumer before the creditor obtains a credit report. A firm offer of credit to the consumer provides this connection. Permitting the practice of screening without this link would be contrary to the purpose of the act.

Bank Safeguards

Banks may use the following controls in developing screened lists:

- The bank may wish to be specific in the credit-granting criteria it designates for targeting creditworthy consumers. This will ensure that the bank is not obligated to extend credit to persons who do not meet its standards. In addition, prompt use of the screened list after receipt from the credit bureau will further ensure that credit is extended only to persons meeting the specified standards.

- The bank may request tiered lists that identify consumers with different characteristics, enabling the bank to make different credit offers (e.g., various credit limits).

- The bank may include demographic analysis, such as data on geography (for example, to establish a service area), income, and type of employment (for example, by the use of specialized magazine subscription lists). This analysis may be applied by the credit bureau or by a third party after the initial screen. The application of demographic analysis must not have the effect of unlawfully excluding persons.

- If the bank wishes to limit the number of consumers to whom it offers credit, it may request the credit bureau or a third party to make random deletions from the list.

In all cases, whether an additional screen is obtained (either demographic or random), the bank must make an offer of credit to all consumers whose names appear on the final screened list.

Offer of Credit

The bank must make a firm offer of credit to all consumers whose names appear on the screened list. A conditional offer of credit is inadequate since it indicates that the bank does not intend to enter into a credit transaction unless the consumer meets a subsequent condition. For example, the imposition of a minimum income requirement on the credit application it provides to consumers on the screened list would not indicate a firm offer of credit.

Withdrawal of an Offer

Once the consumer has accepted the offer of credit, the bank cannot, except in limited circumstances, withdraw or deny the credit, even when the action is based on new information concerning the consumer. Errors in applying the criteria to the data base of the credit bureau during the screening or failure of the screening to retrieve all information about the consumer do not qualify as permissible reasons for withdrawing an offer.

Only in specified and unusual circumstances that occur between the screen and the consumer's acceptance may the bank withdraw an offer of credit. These circumstances include foreclosure, attachment, garnishment, repossession, charge-offs, filing for bankruptcy, or entry of liens or judgments. These criteria must have been part of the original screening to qualify as valid reasons for withdrawing or denying the offer.

The bank may withdraw the offer if it determines that the consumer:

- Is below the age required for a valid contract.

- Has moved beyond the bank's service area for the product offered (if the service area is limited).

- Has fraudulently altered information in the credit report.

Other permissible practices

- The bank may offer initially a modest credit limit and increase it after a full credit report has been obtained, provided the terms of the initial guaranteed credit are clearly specified. A modest credit limit may not be lower than the usual minimum limit offered for a particular product. Once the consumer has accepted the initial credit offer, the bank may request information verifying income to offer a higher credit limit.

- The bank may ask for identifying information (such as the home address and social security number) in the offer of credit.

- The bank may impose a reasonable time limit on the period during which the offer of credit is available. It may treat any response received after the deadline as a regular credit application and may obtain a full credit report to evaluate the consumer's creditworthiness.

- Only when the consumer accepts the credit offer may the bank obtain a full credit report on the consumer. The consumer's account may be reviewed regularly, and if the consumer does not prove to be creditworthy, the bank may close the account.

- The bank may screen using its own records on the bank's previous transactions or experiences with particular consumers without making an offer of credit. Any screening that uses records held by either subsidiaries or affiliates will trigger FCRA coverage.

- The bank may require screened consumers accepting credit offers to create a legal obligation for the credit by, for example, signing a credit contract or security agreement.

OCC Opinion Letters – Fair Credit Reporting Act

October 3, 1979 Letter

This is in response to your memorandum dated June 19, 1979, concerning the national bank. You questioned whether the provisions of the Fair Credit Reporting Act are applicable to the national bank when, pursuant to an agency agreement, the bank transmits credit information about the customers of its affiliates to third parties pursuant to inquiries for such information.

The circumstances in this case were described essentially as follows: the national bank performs EDP services for its affiliate banks by maintaining, e.g., records containing credit information on their customers. The bank also acts as a reference point for the disclosure of all credit data on the customers of those affiliate banks. For instance, if a customer of an affiliate bank applying for credit with a merchant lists that affiliate bank as a credit reference, the merchant is directed by the affiliate to call the national bank. The institution's employees access the general ledger information from the data it stores for that affiliate bank and passes the information directly to the merchant. The caller is required to identify the bank given as a reference and will only receive information regarding that affiliate's experience with the customer. Before disclosing such information for those other banks, the national bank executed with its affiliates an agency agreement which authorizes it to provide such information as an agency for the affiliates.

The Fair Credit Reporting Act (FCRA), 15 USC 1681 et seq., is designed to place disclosure obligations on the users of consumer reports, as well as to provide procedures that insure the relevancy, accuracy and confidentiality of the records maintained by consumer reporting agencies. According to the act,

> [t]he term "consumer reporting agency" means any person which, for monetary fees, dues, or on a cooperative nonprofit basis, regularly engages in whole or in part in the practice of assembling or evaluating consumer credit information or other information on consumers for the purpose of furnishing consumer reports to third parties . . .

15 USC 1681a(f). In its other definitional parts, however, the act excludes from its scope, e.g.

> any report containing information solely as to transactions or experiences between the consumer and the person making the report ... [emphasis added].

15 USC 1681a(d). This statutory language raises the issue of whether the national bank should be considered to be a "consumer reporting agency" that must monitor the accuracy of the reports and the reports' prospective users, resolve consumer disputes relating to the reported information, and keep records of the recipients of information.

Counsel for the national bank maintains that, because of the agency agreement, the bank is not acting as a consumer reporting agency for the purposes of FCRA. In fact, each of the affiliate banks is here forwarding information on its own experience (which is exempted from the coverage of the act), although, for reasons of economy and effectiveness, the affiliates have chosen to employ the national bank as their agent to perform those functions. In support of the bank's position, the counsel has cited Wood v. Holiday Inn Inc., 508 F.2d 167 (5th Cir. 1975). In that case, plaintiff had his credit card revoked by Gulf after attempting to use it to pay for his motel room. Gulf had authorized National Data Corporation (NDC) to indicate to merchants accepting the Gulf credit card whether an extension of credit in individual instances is granted. In Wood, the innkeeper called NDC, and, after being told that credit should not be extended on the card, seized the card. The plaintiff sued Gulf, Holiday Inn, the Holiday Inn franchisee and the innkeeper for negligence regarding the maintenance of the credit data and violations of FCRA. However, the court held that neither Gulf nor Holiday Inn as its representative had violated FCRA.

Further, it has been noted by the national bank's counsel that, within its general powers, 12 USC 24 (7), a national bank is authorized to act as an agent for another person. Thus, to interpret FCRA to apply in this case would be a restriction on the existing powers of the bank. Also, in practical terms, the existing arrangement provides cost-effectiveness and utilization of computer services that the affiliates, acting separately, could not achieve.

On the other hand, the statutory language above exempts an entity from reporting its own experience. Thus, a bank may report only its own credit experience to other financial institutions without becoming a "consumer reporting agency." In 1971, a joint compliance statement issued by the financial regulatory agencies adopted the position that this exception does not apply in a situation where a bank transfers credit information of its affiliates:

16. Is it possible that a financial institution could be a consumer reporting agency?

   Yes. If the financial institution regularly passes on information in its files about a consumer, other than information solely as to its transactions or experiences with the consumer, it may be considered a consumer reporting agency. A consumer reporting agency is any entity which, for monetary fees, dues, or on a cooperative nonprofit basis, regularly engages in whole or in part in the practice of assembling consumer credit information or other information on consumers for the purposes of furnishing consumer reports to third parties, and which uses any means or facility of interstate commerce for the purpose of preparing or furnishing consumer reports (16 CFR 603(d)(f)).

17. Does this apply to the regular exchange of information between correspondent financial institutions, or between a holding company and its subsidiaries, or between subsidiaries of the holding company?

   Yes. However, a branch or department of a financial institution may furnish information to another branch or department of that financial institution without becoming a consumer reporting agency.

Guidelines for Financial institutions in Complying With Fair Credit Reporting Act, May 1971. See also, CCH Consumer Credit Guide 11, 203.

In the past, OCC has explicitly ruled that, despite an existing agency agreement between a bank holding company and its affiliates, the handling of affiliates' credit information, and its reporting to third parties by the bank holding company brought it within the FCRA definition of a "consumer reporting agency." In this case, the national bank and its affiliates are organized under a holding company structure, and the national bank provides the data processing and reporting services for its affiliates. It appears that, in substance, the arrangement is identical to the situation referred to in the memorandum and in the letter.

Further, I cannot agree with the opinion of the bank counsel that Wood v. Holiday Inn, supra, has established a case law precedent exempting an agency relationship from the scope of FCRA. That case does not appear to be on point with the present situation for the following reasons: (1) To be precisely on point, Wood should have discussed the liability of National Data Corporation, which transmitted a credit decision made by Gulf to individual Holiday Inns, upon request. However, NDC was not even sued in this case; (2) Gulf "handled all credit transactions of Holiday Inns" by, among other things, assuming the risk for all charges made at each Inn. Accordingly, Gulf was entitled to make a credit decision (which was not itself a consumer credit report) and used NDC to transmit that decision to any Holiday Inn that received a charge from specific customers. This is entirely different from the relationship between the national bank and its affiliates. (3) In essence, the court opinion discussed whether the innkeeper and Holiday Inn could be regarded as Gulf's agents for the purpose of establishing the tort liability of Gulf for the possible negligence of these parties. In that respect, the opinion does not appear to be directly relevant in considering the scope of FCRA.

Consequently, it is my opinion that the national bank is a "consumer reporting agency" for the purposes of FCRA when it directly transmits credit information of its affiliates to third parties. While I recognize that such an arrangement may well be beneficial and efficient for the financial institutions involved, it nevertheless presents a situation in which FCRA intended to provide protection to consumers, i.e., the reporting of their credit information by a person other than the immediate creditor.

On the other hand, this conclusion can be avoided if the request for credit information will be answered by the affiliate itself. In this case, the national bank may still continue to process and store the credit information for the affiliates. To facilitate compliance, the bank may wish to consider installing a terminal at each affiliate bank so that each affiliate would have access to and direct dominion over the information concerning its customers and could then provide such information to third-party inquirers with considerable speed and accuracy while still taking advantage of the cost benefits of using the main national bank computer. Again, it must be emphasized that to avoid becoming a consumer reporting agency, the national bank must not pass on to an affiliate information other than that appearing in the records of the affiliate in question.

June 15, 1987 Letter

You have asked whether a national bank can provide a consumer's loan application and trade references (list of consumer creditors other than the bank) to a credit bureau "for verification" without the bank thereby becoming a "consumer reporting agency" subject to the restrictions and responsibilities imposed by the Fair Credit Reporting Act (FCRA). The Federal Trade Commission (FTC) staff (in a letter dated May 2, 1986) and the Federal Reserve Board (FRB) staff (in a letter dated September 3, 1986) have recently decided this question in the affirmative. Likewise, we conclude that as long as a bank is providing information solely for verification in order to reach a decision on a pending credit application, the bank can do so without becoming a consumer reporting agency under the FCRA.

One of the purposes of the Fair Credit Reporting Act, 15 USC 1681 et seq., is to regulate the types of information that can be gathered about a consumer and distributed by entities involved in the credit application process. The restrictions regarding dissemination of information about consumers apply to "consumer reporting agencies." A consumer reporting agency is defined by the act as:

> any person which, for monetary fees, dues, or on a cooperative nonprofit basis, regularly engages in whole or in part in the practice of assembling or evaluating consumer credit information or other information on consumers for the purpose of furnishing consumer reports to third parties, and which uses any means or facility of interstate commerce for the purpose of preparing or furnishing consumer report. (15 USC 1681a(f)) (Emphasis added.)

A consumer report is defined as:

> any written, oral, or other communication of any information by a consumer reporting agency bearing on a consumer's creditworthiness, credit standing, credit capacity, character, general reputation, personal characteristics, or mode of living which is used or expected to be used or collected in whole or in part for the purpose of serving as a factor in establishing the consumer's eligibility for (1) credit or insurance to be used primarily for personal, family, or household purposes, or (2)

employment purposes, or (3) other purposes authorized under section 1681b of this title. (15 USC 1681a(d)) (Emphasis added.)

A determination of the appropriate coverage of the act is difficult because of the circularity of the quoted definitions. Accordingly, one must look beyond the language of the provisions to their substance. The clear intent of the FCRA is to reach those entities that are in the business of gathering information about consumers to be used by third parties in making credit decisions.

In the situation presented, banks gather information directly from particular consumers on their own loan application forms. They would like to forward some (trade references) or all (the entire loan application) of this information to a third party (credit bureau) for verification in connection with their own use of the information in reaching a credit decision. The banks do not receive any fees in such transactions; in fact, they pay the credit bureau a fee for verifying the data. The information transmitted appears to fit the definition of "consumer report," in that trade references and other data from loan applications do bear on one or more of the characteristics listed in the statute (creditworthiness, credit standing, credit capacity, etc.) if the transmitter is a "consumer reporting agency."

Thus, the critical issue is whether the "credit report" is being disseminated by a "consumer reporting agency." The definition of "consumer reporting agency" contains four elements:

- Transmission for a fee, or on a cooperative nonprofit basis.

- By a person regularly engaged in the practice of assembling or evaluating consumer credit information or other information on consumers.

- For the purpose of furnishing consumer reports to third parties.

- Through interstate means.

See, e.g., Porter v. Talbot Perkins Children's Services, 355 F. Supp. 174, 176-77 (S.D.N.Y. 1973). If one of these elements is absent from a transaction, the transmitter falls outside the definition and, thus, is not a "consumer reporting agency."

In the case at hand, the bank does not appear to furnish the consumer report for a fee or on a nonprofit cooperative basis. Furthermore, the information is forwarded for the purpose of verification rather than for the purpose of furnishing consumer reports to third parties. Thus, the initiator of such a transaction seems to fall outside the statutory definition of a "consumer reporting agency". However, if the bank paid a lower fee for such verification reports than for general credit reports that were requested without providing consumer information and if such lower fees were not justified by lower costs but, in fact, were a form of compensation for the information provided, a different case would be presented.

As noted above, this conclusion is consistent with the position taken by other agencies. Moreover, it is not inconsistent with recent statements of this Office. In a letter dated December 1, 1971, the FRB appeared to opine that a state member bank distributing credit and trade references to a credit bureau would be a consumer reporting agency. In 1984, OCC received a request to essentially disapprove that informal FRB interpretation on two grounds. These were, first, that credit and trade references are not "information" under the FCRA and, second, that under such circumstances, the bank and the credit bureau are "joint users" of the credit and trade references and thus should be treated as a combination analogous to joint creditors. In Interpretative Letter No. 335, April 9, 1985, reprinted in, [Current] Federal Banking Law Rep. (CCH), ¶85,505, Charles F. Byrd, Assistant Director, LASD, rejected these two arguments and, thus, seemed to imply that OCC would follow the 1971 FRB letter. However, it is my opinion that the OCC letter merely rejected the specific arguments advanced and did not address the more general issue.

Subsequently, the FTC addressed the issue in a May 3, 1986, letter. In deciding whether the transmission of application information to a credit bureau for verification would render a creditor a "consumer reporting agency," the FTC looked to the definition of consumer agency contained in the act. It said:

> A party that furnishes consumer reports must meet all five elements of the definition – compensation (monetary fees ...), extent (regularly ...), activity (assembling or evaluating ...), purpose (for the purpose of furnishing consumer reports to third parties), and use of interstate commerce – in order to be classified as a "consumer reporting agency." In the scenario you posed, it is quite clear that the compensation

requirement of the definition would not be met ... Instead of receiving payment or interacting with the credit bureau on a cooperative nonprofit basis, the creditor would be paying the credit bureau to verify the information in the application and to provide the creditor a consumer report for use in deciding whether to grant or deny the application. Because that first critical element of the definition (compensation) is clearly not present, it is our opinion that the creditor would not be a "consumer reporting agency" in the situation you described. Furthermore, we note that the creditor's purpose (as you have described it) in providing applications to the credit bureau is not to "(furnish) consumer reports to third parties," but rather to obtain from the credit bureau consumer reports containing information that will enable the creditor to evaluate its own potential risk in extending credit to the applicants.

Likewise, in a letter dated September 3, 1986, FRB staff reached the same conclusion and said that a state member bank is not a consumer reporting agency under the FCRA when it transmits a credit applicant's credit and trade references or other information from a credit application to a credit bureau in order to have the information verified and a consumer report issued.

I agree with the reasoning of the other agencies and, additionally, believe that a uniform position should be maintained. Accordingly, we conclude that a national bank that transmits consumer credit information to a credit bureau should not be deemed to be a consumer reporting agency when it does so only for purposes of obtaining verification of that information for a credit report.

March 15, 1989 Letter

This is in response to your letter dated January 26, 1989, regarding the applicability of the Fair Credit Reporting Act (FCRA), 15 USC 1681 et seq., to the proposal described below.

BHC through its subsidiary banks and affiliate nonbanks (hereinafter referred to as "subsidiary" or "subsidiaries") offers a variety of services and products to its customers. Currently, a customer seeking the subsidiaries' financial services and products has to fill out a separate application for each one. The

BHC seeks to make these services and products available to its customers in a more efficient manner by permitting customers to provide information on a single application that, at their written request, would be forwarded to the designated subsidiaries.[1] There would be no fee for this service, and the application would be forwarded simply by photocopying it and transmitting the photocopied application to the designated subsidiaries. The information forwarded would not be interpreted, summarized, assembled, or evaluated in any way.

The FCRA concerns, among other things, the reporting of consumer reports by consumer reporting agencies. A consumer report is defined as:

> (d)...any written, oral, or other communication of any information by a consumer reporting agency bearing on a consumer's credit-worthiness, credit standing, credit capacity, character, general reputation, personal characteristics, mode of living which is used or expected to be used or collected in whole or in part for the purpose of serving as a factor in establishing the consumer's eligibility for (1) credit or insurance to be used primarily for personal, family, or household purposes, or (2) employment purposes, or (3) other purposes authorized under section 1681b of this title. ... [15 USC 1681(d) (Emphasis added.)]

A consumer reporting agency is defined as:

> any person which, for monetary fees, dues, or on a cooperative nonprofit basis, regularly engages in whole or in part in the practice of assembling or evaluating consumer credit information or other information on consumers for the purpose of furnishing consumer reports to third parties, and which uses any means or facility of interstate commerce for the purpose of preparing or furnishing consumer reports. 15 USC 1681a(f) (Emphasis added.)

The definition of a "consumer reporting agency" contains four elements: (1) transmission for a fee or on a cooperative nonprofit basis; (2) regularly engaged in the practice of assembling or evaluating credit information; (3) for

---

[1] However, a customer would not be prohibited from filling out an application form for each of the BHC's subsidiaries, instead of completing a single form for all or some of the subsidiaries.

the purpose of furnishing consumer reports to third parties; and (4) through interstate commerce. If one of these elements is absent from the transaction, the transmitter falls outside the definition and, thus, is not a consumer reporting agency. See, e.g., Porter v. Talbot Perkins Children's Services, 355 F. Supp. 174, 176-77 (S.D.N.Y. 1973)

You have represented that the subsidiaries will not be assembling or evaluating a customer's credit information before it is transmitted to the affiliated subsidiary. The concept of assembling or evaluating consumer credit information implies a function which involves more than the receipt and retransmission of information. See, e.g., D'Angelo v. Wilmington Medical Center Inc., 515 F. Supp. 1250, 1253 (D.De.1981). Accordingly, it appears that the subsidiaries would not be consumer reporting agencies under the FCRA.[2]

Further, it appears that the FCRA should not apply to a situation where a consumer specifically requests that a credit application be transmitted to another entity. Congress' purpose in enacting the FCRA was to provide a means for the accurate, efficient, and fair reporting of credit information while insuring impartiality and a respect for the consumer's right to privacy. See 15 USC 1681. The FCRA was designed to "protect consumers from inaccurate or arbitrary information in a consumer report which is being used as a factor in determining an individual's eligibility for credit, insurance, or employment." 116 Cong. Reg. 36572 (1970)

The evils that the FCRA was designed to prevent do not exist where information is directly provided by the consumer to the subsidiary and at his/her written request the information, without assembly or evaluation, is transmitted to an affiliated entity. In that case, the consumer is assured that the information is accurate and fair because he/she directly provided it. Also, because the information has not been assembled or evaluated by the subsidiary, the consumer is assured that the application will be impartial. Finally, because the consumer specifically requested in writing that the application be transmitted to other subsidiaries, the consumer is assured of his/her right of privacy. Accordingly, it appears that the FCRA does not apply in this instant case.

---

[2] However, you should note that if a customer's application were to be evaluated before its transmission to an affiliated subsidiary, then the transmitting subsidiary would be considered a "consumer reporting agency" under the FCRA.

Moreover, in cases where a customer's application form is transmitted to another subsidiary for the same type of credit, the Federal Trade Commission's proposed commentary to the FCRA recognizes that the parties to the information would be "joint users" and thus not credit reporting agencies. In this regard, the commentary states:

8. Joint Users of Consumer(s) Reports

Entities that share consumer reports with others that are jointly involved in decisions for which there are permissible purposes to obtain the reports may be "joint users" rather than consumer reporting agencies. For example, if a lender forwards consumer reports...to another creditor for use in considering a consumer's loan application at the consumer's request, the lender does not become a consumer reporting agency by virtue of such action ... 53 Fed. Reg. 29696, 29703 (Aug. 8, 1988.) (Emphasis added.)

Accordingly, where the application is transmitted at the request of the consumer, the subsidiaries would not be considered consumer reporting agencies under the FCRA.

Laws

15 USC 1681, Fair Credit Reporting Act

Regulations

16 CFR 600, Statements of General Policy or Interpretations under the Fair Credit Reporting Act

OCC Issuances

Examining Circular 263, SMS Documentation Policy